IN THE EYE OF THE ELEPHANT

IN THE EYE

of the

ELEPHANT

Poems

Moira Magneson

SIXTEEN RIVERS PRESS

Printed in the United States of America

Published by Sixteen Rivers Press
P.O. Box 640663
San Francisco, CA 94164
www.sixteenrivers.org

LCCN: 2025930173
ISBN: 978-1-939639-37-0

Cover photo: iStock/Ahmad Mufti
Author photo: Anmarie Fielding Weeks
Book design: Wayne Smith

for Eric

CONTENTS

III

I

I stand and look at them long and long.

—Walt Whitman

CONFESSION

I am having an affair
with the mule next door
everything about him
dazzles   long black
tail swishing his backside
like a broom scattering
flies and dust   his corded
muscled neck pushing
me along the fence   his eyes
dark with spite and sorrow.
Early mornings before the light
we rendezvous   I tramp
the tall grass and thistle
to the corner of our land
where he greets me
gentle mouth nuzzling
my sugared hand. Usually
I am content just to be
near him   but sometimes
the urge to climb inside
his body is unbearable.
We are both mongrels born
to parents worlds apart
lineage a cul-de-sac   saddled
with our onliness   we understand
our ending   how it finishes here
in this field   suffering each other

madly   in love with apples sugar words
in wind   the scent of earth and heaven.

THIS HOUND

for Creek

Wherever scent blows, this hound goes. Flop-eared
mutt, three times snake-bit, bound by the black
wet leather of his nose. He trots

the trail happily, lapping the green
hills over & back again. *O!* to be
this dog, pissing & crapping, drinking

in the trough of wind—coyote scat,
deer fur snagged on outcrop rock,
pine duff, the frag & slough

of opossum skin, the bear's
bleached bones, musky underneath
of river stone—

this swoon of smells his canine art,
rotting offal the pleasure of his days.
Unlike me, he loves

this stinking world.
With all his wagging heart
he barks rough praise.

COCKEYED

I ride for hours
in the Woody with my father.
He makes a kind of music
with beer bottles
held against the wind.
Just us, no one else.
He pulls over often to pee.
Finally, we stop at a field,
get out of the car.
C'mon, he says.
On the barbed wire fence—
the bleached husk of a cat.
The smell is wonderful!
I try to touch,
he pulls me away.
Mary Quince Qually,
a blue-and-white beagle,
is in my arms.
Stickers in my red socks.
A man walks out of the corn,
hugs my father, looks down at me
with one eye.
There is no other.
Elephants in the sky.
Mary Quince Qually growls.
The stranger lifts and spins
me in the dusk. I can see

a long, long way, to the hump
of highway and beyond
to a line where all light ends.
I look into his blue marble.
Where the other eye
should have been,
I poke my finger—smooth skin.
Where's your eye?
He laughs. *A rooster pecked it out.*
Moira, my father says,
Give your grandfather a kiss.
My socks are red.
I can count to four.
Mary Quince Qually
doesn't like this man.

OWLING

The naturalist took us owling
at twilight up in the green hills
of American Canyon. I knew

the place—a deep cleft in the land   horse
stables   dairies. We stopped
at a stand of eucalyptus. A fine

rain coming down. I could hear the river
of cars running parallel on the interstate—
swoosh   swoosh   swoosh

We were told a great horned owl lived
nearby high in the oily   bushy   menthol.
I scanned the treetops.

The man pulled a little bundle from his trouser
pocket—a field mouse tethered
with a long leash of string.

Anchored to a heavy stone
the tiny creature took off
scurrying to the end of her world

where she stopped short   quaking. Our guide
giddy with the certain telos
of his design   the owl descending

from his perch   a terrible winged minotaur. But there
on the earth   tangled in twine   the bird also
suffered   whirlwind gathered up

with leather gloves   metal band crimped
on his leg   identified   accounted for   let go.
I turned   walked back to the truck   got in

huddled on the passenger side   waited
and wondered for all our lives—what marvels
we were   wild   innocent   damned.

AFTER THE ELECTION

The morning star blazes in the sky

as I walk up my road. The sharp smell of dung
          trailing the air. A kind
of incense. At the hillcrest a band of brindled goats.
Each scumbling in its own cloud
                    of steam. Each heart,
lit by its own lamp.

Their little tails tremble furiously
at my approach. What have I
          to offer but empty hands?
Still they lick my fingers with their gravelly tongues.
          Heads cocked. Gauging.

Let me slip though their pupils' black
                              keyhole slit
and I will scamper in their scrum of bleat and fur.
                  I will follow.
Skip the wet rocky earth with cloven feet.
                              I will wager
          all my sins
for this: Patch of green grass.
    Comfort of the swollen teat. Hot sweet
milk of the known
                  and unknown world.

BODHISATTVA

old black cat napping
beneath the blossoming plum
humming with the bees

APPARITION

High in the Sawtooths   the wind   the wind
tugged me from sleep and I slipped
from the skein of my down bag.

I walked to the river   crossed the wild
alphabet of scattered stone and sat with back against
the scratch of a driftwood pine. Stars salted the sky.

The campfire's orange-embered eye   watching.

I nodded off   then woke   shivering to see the antlered crown break
the water   enormous muscled shadow rising
slowly   slowly   into his own weather.

Huffing white clouds of steam   water rivering off
the dewlap   he ascended the bank to the meadow   past
the miners' cabins   the scabbed orchard where

he nosed the fallen apples but did not eat.   I saw him
move   up and up   a shaggy darkness parting the trees
disappearing into the forest.   I saw

and though I was left cold and alone   and though I would walk
to the campfire   feed it   till it burned hot and furious
though I would make breakfast   go on with my life

some part of me was gone   surrendered to that form
          vanished with him into the wild dark.
That much I understood.

EYE AND THE ELEPHANT

When I despair, which is often these days,
for this fractious world so bent
upon itself, I go back
to that Sunday morning in Chitwan,
wood smoke scenting November air.
Alone and walking a footpath
to the river, I come to a clearing
where I spot a mahout and his elephant.
Catching my stare, he beckons me
to their side. Soon, I am feeding her banana leaves.
She smells dusty and sweet. Her pink-mottled ears—
deckle-edged, ragged—flap. I pat her skin,
its rough, warm comfort, then look into her eye,
her right eye, so brown and deep it seems
steeped in sorrow. Her gaze a transom to my self,
my heart a pail holding moon and stars.
I am speaking the language of elephants. And then,
a miracle! She lets down her trunk. Lightfooted,
I climb that great leather ladder, traverse
the landscape of hide and shoulder, until
I'm straddling her, my toes brushing her ears.
We walk together—such magnificent gentle steps!
Hatti Hatti mero saathi.
And I am content—rocking, rocking—
just behind her domed forehead,
high in the clouds, dust rising
from the ancient earth.

Hatti Hatti mero saathi. O noble being!
How beautiful to be cradled in the heart
of the world. *O elephant!*

HIPPOPOTAMUS: AN INSERTED PROPOSITION

(Is there a rhinoceros in the room? One of the earliest encounters between Bertrand Russell and the young Ludwig Wittgenstein involved a discussion about whether there was a rhinoceros in their room. Apparently, when Wittgenstein 'refused to admit that it was certain that there was not a rhinoceros in the room,' Russell half-jokingly looked underneath the desks to prove it. But to no avail. 'My German engineer, I think, is a fool,' concluded Russell. 'He thinks nothing empirical is knowable—I asked him to admit that there was not a rhinoceros in the room, but he wouldn't.')
—J. F. MacDonald, "Russell, Wittgenstein, and the Problem of the Rhinoceros"

Mudwallower—tusked herbivore,
fierce creature of the occipital
cranial—tramples a poem's
ground of existence, big rump
rubbing its margins.

Pthpthpthpthpthpthpthpthpthpth.

There! Do you hear him?

Pthpthpthpthpthpthpthpthpthpth.P
thpthpthpthpthpthpthpthpthpth.Pt
hpthpthpthpthpthpthpthpthpth.Pth
pthpthpthpthpthpthpthpthpth.Pthp
thpthpthpthpthpthpthpthpth.Pthpt
hpthpthpthpthpthpthpthpth.Pthpth
pthpthpthpthpthpthpthpth.Pthpthp
thpthpthpthpthpthpthpth.Pthpthpt
hpthpthpthpthpthpthpth.Pthpthpth
pthpthpthpthpthpthpth.Pthpthpthp

thpthpthpthpthpthpth.Pthpthpthpt
hpthpthpthpthpthpth.Pthpthpthpth
pthpthpthpthpthpth.Pthpthpthpthp
thpthpthpthpthpth.Pthpthpthpthpt
hpthpthpthpthpth.Pthpthpthpthpth
pthpthpthpthpth.Pthpthpthpthpthp
thpthpthpthpth.Pthpthpthpthpthpt
hpthpthpthpth.Pthpthpthpthpthpth
pthpthpthpth.Pthpthpthpthpthpthp
thpthpthpth.Pthpthpthpthpthpthpt
hpthpthpth.Pthpthpthpthpthpthpth

Go on! You heard him. He just shat.
And peed. Now the poem is wet
with hippopotamus. I tell you
there is only so much heft
and weight a poem can take.

(A crown sonnet can house a hippo, but
trust me, a villanelle—hell.)

Ah! Aroma! The redolent indolence
of a certain hippopotamus: Never mind
the certainty of the hippopotamus in
this poem

chewing on the fallen fruit of logos,
the long lianas of lines. Tromping
tercets, headbutting stanzas off the page.

He can do and undo everything.

Look! Over there! At the watering hole:
he has got himself into quite an enjamb—
ment—hippopotamus/hippo-
potamus.

O my! There are two hippopotamuses
in this poem.

They are rutting! Engaged
in their fat frisson of excitement!

O! O! O! O! O! O! O! O! O! O! O! O!

Dear reader, voyeur,
you are disturbing
them. The hippopotami
would now like you
to quietly excuse yourself,
take your feeble, flimsy
inner tube of language, kick
downriver with your puny
legs and over the falls
to the crocodiles . . .

SUNDAY

Eighteen-wheeler on Highway 99 rattles along
in the slow lane, stinking of shit and loaded
with lowing cattle, pink muzzles pressed
to perforated panels. On their way
to the house of revelations where crowded
together, they smell him before they meet him.
Bellowing out hosannas, each files up the ramp
to the end of the story: God is a man
swinging a sledgehammer, apron slick with blood.
When his shift is done, another man just like him
will step up to take his place.

REQUIEM

This fall, every day on my way to work, I see
the slaughtered bucks slumped along the roadside,
huge dun-colored bodies stilled, the urgency
that summoned them long gone. Each animal I pass
I praise. And though I don't believe, I say
a prayer—*God bless*—as if words were a bridge
they could clatter across, continuing on,
following the delicious tang and heat
of love, as if they could still couple, complete
themselves in the ecstasy each of us desires, as if
words could be something more than syllables
ghosting air on a dark November morning.

THANKSGIVING

I find the shrew mole in November,
lying on the brick, cloaked with cold,
out of his element. His fur thick,
dark as a raincloud.

I lie down beside him and believe
he's swimming now above his body,
coarse paws paddling the air, a draught
of stench eddying behind.

Surely he has lingered long enough
to have seen that other genus of laborers
who so love the earth arrive, equipped
with pickaxes and shovels.

How quickly they work at the business
of transcendence, entering the mouth
and sphincter like they are entering
the tunnel of love.

Look how they undress him, blindly
caress his treasures: the tender palate,
the slick chute of the rectum,
the rich, stalled hemoglobin.

His sweetbread their leaven;
through him they'll birth

into their wings and rise,
bear him up to wind, to sky.

I praise the dead and the living, all I am given.
I praise *Earth as it is*, its holy cup my heaven.

HERSELF

I have written a poem about an ecstatic
experience I once had looking into the eye
of an elephant. I rode her suffering deep
into the forest, the way she and others like her
have been ridden for centuries. I had thought
the poem was about the elephant, but truly
it was not. The elephant was nowhere
in the poem, only a semblance of the great,
sad creature I saw. Somehow, I imagined
I could put her back together with words.
Why can't her bones rest?
Why must I resurrect her? What else
can the poem be but a boxcar, a cage,
an arena where she performs all day,
a melancholy shuffle under the weight
of idea, the long prod and hook of words,
my desire to make her noble, magnificent.
And look, here come the readers, peering in,
brutal in their innocence, their wish to belong
to something bigger than themselves.
What exchange is this—a pound, a ten-spot
for her misery? Such cruel economy.
Let the big top fall, the lines go slack.
Let my words swirl like dust.
Let her amble to the muddy river
where she can roll and bathe with her kin.
All she ever wanted to be was herself.

THE VANISHING

once there was
    you, sweet pika,
        thick pelt & saucer ears

tiny tumble
    of energy
        scampering over

Sierra rock
    gathering grass seed
        & forget-me-nots

when the summers
    grew too long
        & cruel you fled

to higher cooler ground
    & when the heat
        grew hotter still

you fled again
    again again
        until there was

no more fleeing
    no more mountain
        to climb

only the sky's
blue grieving
holding you

in its boundless gaze
before your
final leaving

II

Good morning heartache, sit down.

—Billie Holiday

CURRICULUM VITAE

I have slept under
overpasses, in graveyards,
on the drunken night bus
to Nepal. I have tricked
psychiatrists, abandoned
friends, even babies,
as easily as changing clothes.
I have hitchhiked
from Idaho to Stockton,
wearing nearly nothing at all.
I have leapt
into a rolling boxcar,
made a bed of pissy cardboard
& lain on it. I have spun
my Dodge Dart 360 degrees
in rush hour traffic
on the way
to my lover, a married man.
I have betrayed
more women than men
even though
more men than women
have betrayed me. I was
seam-ripped by a man
when I was four.
I've had a knife to my neck,
negotiated for my life

in the backseat of a big rig.
I have stayed awake three days straight jacked
on speed & seen my mind
wander the world without me.
I'm all that.

PERFECT

It was Christmas. The "Dance of the Sugar Plum Fairies" played
on the console. All around the room I twirled in my pink tutu   d i z z y
with my own magnificence. Until they took off my clothes. Stuck me
in her black leather riding boots. Posed me for the camera. *Smile*, they said,
as if you have a secret   as if you've done something bad.

In the photograph—hands on hips   pelvis tipped—I might as well be
a four-year-old dominatrix. Boots riding the tops of my thighs.
Underscoring the thin seam of my vulva. I'm smiling. Happy to make them
happy. At last. I liked how they gasped and giggled on the couch.

Off stage. Out of the picture. The neighbor waited. Finding me alone
one afternoon   he pulled me into the alley. Promising a surprise. He took
everything off but my shoes. Then   in the way my father taught me
to slip a black olive onto my thumb   he tried me on for size.

HOW I GREW UP

in memoriam Lisa Anne Beery (1958–1974)

i

At fifteen I was taught how to walk in Oakland
walk like you could beat   the shit
out of anybody
walk with a scream   head high
NEVER   at   night
away from   trees   cars   men

My friend who was also fifteen
never grew older   she was stripped of her clothes
fucked   and as she was fucked   strangled
          buried   on a hill   crowded
with eucalyptus and
five other women

ii

You   live
on that pink scar of land in the bay
  San Quentin
a corridor leads to a corridor
leads to another   turn right
and there is the longest corridor of all

That's where you stay
in a cell to yourself

Occasionally you are let out
and you go to the wood shop
where you finish a cabinet of bird's-eye maple

you like to work with your hands

There is another room   you know it
an arena
where the Minotaur
flips you over its head
in a golden vibrant moment

I could watch you go dead

EXCAVATION

And if I went
to your grave
in Freedom,
broke the earth
with a pickaxe,
then shoveled
dirt day and night—
for however long
it took to get
to the box,
and if I ripped
out the nails
with a hammer's claw,
pried open the rotting
plywood to see
beetles scatter
from the nightgowned bones,
and if I saw the rings
on your fingers,
one for the man who made
my mother, the other
for the man who followed,
and if I pulled you up
by your shoulders
so that your hollow
sockets faced mine,
and if I could peer

into the dark
mindshaft, see
the girl alone
in the house
for weeks, who fends
off your fists
and knives, who dreams
of leaping horses,
and if I might
call to her—
Olly oxen free—
if I could hear
her breathing,
and if I could turn
you upside down
and shake her out
of your absence
so that she might
fall into my palm,
if I could gaze
into that bright gem
of emptiness—
Nancy Marie, eight years old—
as a woman might gaze
into her infant's eyes,
what then?

HE DRANK BECAUSE

Jerry & Johnny's was just down the street, because newspapermen
all drink first thing in the morning—good ones, that is—Patterson,
Murphy, Bronson—it was boring not to—they'd heard of
Wadsworth, the convert who'd hightailed it to Salt Lake, dried up, and now
was the most tiresome man on earth. He drank to have fun—

it made him funny, he could tell stories and everybody—hippies,
starlets, politicians, whores, stevedores, gangsters,
revolutionaries—would roar with laughter, and laughter,
like drinking, made him feel warm. He drank

because of his kids: Because the oldest excelled at baseball but was
failing school, doomed to mediocrity; because he and a photographer,
both drunk, had chased his daughter's pet squirrel around her room,
accidentally snapping off its tail, and thus it fell to him, the task
of telling his daughter about death; because the police had picked up
his youngest son, passed out on gin, in the parking lot
of Freeway Variety. He drank

because his wife drove him to drink, because she nagged him not to
and worked two jobs since all their money was spent on his drinking.
He drank because he was angry—

at least twice a week the neighbor's collie crapped on the lawn and
he'd step in it; because his editors had it in for him, his stories buried
on page 22; because his mother's fiancé was five years younger
than him; because his best friend with the beautiful family ran

a hose from the exhaust pipe to the interior of his station wagon and
it was all so much shit on his shoe, and

he yelled at his wife, hit his kids—who could blame him, no one
understood him—why he drank—least of all himself; and so,
admitting that, he drank because there was no way out

of the hard stuff—reporter's notebook flipped open to the woman
whose husband and child had atomized at a railroad crossing,
the arson fire where he lost his footing on a baby charred
into the floor—he drank because

the bandanna knotted around his face did nothing to keep out the stench
of 900 people stacked five bodies deep in the green swelter of Jonestown;
because once he had been a good man but had seen too much and now hated

having to tell the shrink exactly when, where, how, and why
he had been drinking, hated having to see a shrink in the first place
and confess that he couldn't ever forget

his young mother, late at night, laughing, trying on men like they were
ballroom dresses; or his twelve-year-old daughter at the dinner table matter-of-
factly recounting how the neighbor fucked her when she was four—what kind
of father was he, where had he been, at the bar, drinking? He sobbed
to the shrink that he drank because

he knew he was alone, because at last he understood how they could easily
do without him but he couldn't live without them, and he didn't want them
to hate him for drinking, the way he hated his father. He drank because

when he was ten—the day his father walked out on them—his dad poured him his first drink, and said, *Here, little man, the cure for what ails you*, and they laughed.

He drank because it was like love.

LOSING IT

here's what I remember:

my parents had gone off
to Tahiti or some such place to continue
the argument of marriage.

I was upstairs in the bedroom of my boyfriend's house, the television
was on. out the window
I could see
the gray rooftops
of Oakland
the fog strolling down avenues, confident as a dog off leash.

I was seventeen.
in five days
I'd be away at college. it was about time
I did something
with my life.

downstairs
my boyfriend—
not really a boy
but a man—
a machinist
I'd met
at the plant where I worked

was opening

the front door.

Nixon

was scowling on TV

hands clenching

the podium

his wife

his daughters

and their husbands

stood near him

straight-backed.

the presidential seal

sparkled

in the camera light

he went on

about the constitutional

process

about the interests

of the nation

(*yeah, right,* I thought)

how he'd never

been a quitter

and then

I knew!

I bolted

down the stairs

the President's quitting!!!

I yelled to my boyfriend and the two men who sat with him

at the dining room table

a pile

of white powder

in front of them

mounded high on some foxy woman's ass

pictured on the jacket of an Ohio Players album.

this is history!

I blurted as

one man swept his nose along a mirror

they stared

as if I were crazy

I stared

right back

the other man whistled shook his head

brother better watch yourself

he said

she's green.

later in bed we smoked some hash

listened to Richard Pryor

riff

about how stiff and formal white folks were

and then we were kissing

sucking each other's lips and tongues shirts pulled over

heads

jeans tugged off

hips

I traced the ragged scar along his thigh

he licked my neck

and then

he was climbing

on top of me

eyes locked into mine

but I couldn't

do it my mind

swirling

I was lost my head

rolling away from my body

like a marble

an aggie

a milky

as my father would say

pocked

and white

as the moon

a magnolia

sad

as Pat Nixon's face
watching her husband
saying goodbye
to the White House
lost
vanishing
like the white
powder
from the mirror

white
as the girl kneeling over the gunned-down Kent State boy
arms outstretched in horror
white
like my skin *skin tight*
I was
no kind of

bad bad missus driving blind men into ditches
I was white
a joke
a virgin
uptight
just like Richard Pryor said.

what's wrong with me?
I cried
hey hey baby it's okay he soothed

stroking my cheek
winding my hair
around his hand
like a spindle
another time.

and then we talked about my leaving in a week
he teased
you'll fall in love with some white boy
no I won't
we'll never see each other again you'll forget all about me
not true
so we made a bet shook on it
then laughing fell asleep.

that morning I woke
alone—
he had the early shift—
drove home packed for school
a different life

of course
he won the bet we didn't see
each other after that
and I did fall in love with a white boy—
a whole string of them
but I never did forget.

MOM DRIVES FAST

like a rocket down I-80
three kids packed in the back of the Mustang   Naugahyde seats
ashtrays crammed   Jed mutters *Mays*   *McCovey*   *Jesus Alou*
shuffles trading cards   Sean exhales in my face breath rancid last night's beans
mashed into his braces   the top is down our eyes slits in the wind
in & out of twilight traffic we zoom   60   70   85
Mom drives fast redgreengold neon spills onto a blue planet
SHERWIN-WILLIAMS COVER THE EARTH   cattails catch
the sun's last light   Mom veers onto the MacArthur   fartstink
of East Bay MUD   *who let one?*   down by the docks 100-foot-high
loading cranes   white Trojan horses   wait for container ships   Mom
chainsmokes flicks cigarettes like sticks of dynamite out the car
litterbug Sean wails   *shut up* Mom yells   whips by the California Hotel
where eye-level to the freeway   boxed in a gold halo   a man
in his underwear opens a refrigerator   *Muhammad Ali Muhammad Ali* Jed chants
    shut the fuck up your dad's in jail again
again?   it's news to me but everything's news in this family
we careen off Grand   boom boom boom   through three yellow lights
along Lake Merritt past the aviary   nightsong of wrecked birds
past Fairyland   princesses & dwarves   up Franklin into Chinatown
our lungs swelling with the sweet bloom of fortune cookies
fly down 14th the House of Woodwinds the ticking dark face of the Tribune tower
onto Broadway Mexicali Rose Swan's Department Store Rudy's Bail Bonds
to the steps of the jail where she swerves to the curb & brakes
our heads snapping to attention   at the top of the stairs

hands shoved into jingling pockets he waits whistling
& while she holds back we tumble   out   bound   forward
thrilled to prop him up with our love

AT MARTIN ANGEL'S

When it was bad we took your truck and bourbon
drove north   Oregon   hardly speaking at all
    cut the Siskiyous to the Umpqua River
followed a dusty road to its end
Martin Angel's land   there   a hot springs
he had told us about years ago   he had said
    if you're in love   go there

We stripped and stepped into the scald
of that pool   as we sat buoyed
in the water   sweating   I thought
we might have bloomed   your face
ruddy as if scraped
I thought I saw the meanness of years
lift from us   the way a bat   rises
    softly   from a flower or a wound

By dusk your breath was warm with bourbon
you went to start the truck and I walked
a trail to the Umpqua   I almost dove
but stopped   I smelled rot   across the water

    a deer netted in the rocks   the purple
    dunnage of guts drifting   out its side

The truck horn sounded

the legs dangled just enough in the water
so that the current caught its hooves   causing
it to kick now and again
a sort of peculiar   palsied   trot

I had to leave.

DEATH DELUXE

Death came to me this afternoon,
pulled up in his beige station wagon.
His Dobermans leapt out a side door
window and were all over my yard
pissing and crapping like they never
had it so good.

Death pushed his great heft
from behind the wheel,
stood up, wheezed, looked my yard over.
"I've come to mow your lawn," he said.

My lawn was green and downy,
a galaxy of dandelions, weeds.
I liked it overgrown.
"It doesn't need mowing," I told him.
The sun was shining but somehow
all the charm had gone out of the day.

He smiled, and wouldn't you know it,
he had a tooth with a gold star.
"Hey," he grunted. "It's free. You don't get much
for free these days."
He had a point.

"Well, call off those dogs," I said.
"They're making a mess."

Death obliged by whistling, and *ppphhhttt*, like that,
those dogs dissolved mid-piss.
I was impressed.

Then I watched Death do a number
on my yard. With his lawnmower
he cut tunnels, corridors, passages
in the grass, exquisite as an Elizabethan maze.
I was stunned by his skill, his artistry.
Despite his bulk, he really was a handsome fellow.

"It's wonderful," I cried.
"How can I repay you?"
"It's free," he said again, then nodded my way.
"But step down off your porch, come to me."
He had eyes like blue glass.

"You beautiful bitch," he said. Then Death
French-kissed me, got down on all fours.
"Say my name," he growled, and I did
as I was told: "Prince of Darkness. Prince of Fire. Suicide."

Death became wiry, lean. A cock
sprang from his spine like a fin. I crawled
onto his back, straddled him, and we flew.

And I was in love, in love, a little girl
with my best dress on, and we flew,
and oh, what an animal we made.

WORK

I am writing the poem as I punch
my time card. I am writing the poem
as I rouge my nipples, black-rim my eyes.
I am writing the poem as Nikki, Carlotta,
Brandi, and Dawn twirl and chat
in the hall of mirrors—it's dangerous
to use each other's real names. Most days
I am writing the poem as a blonde, sometimes
as a redhead (Midge), once
in a blue moon as a boy,
stuffed in tight-whites, hair butch-waxed back,
swaggering in Doc Martens,
sex-moshing on stage.
When the man with a fondness for Hawaiian
shirts mistakes lap dancing for
love, parks his late model Camry (Barney stickers)
on my street three weeks running, you can bet
every day I am writing the poem. I am still
writing the poem when my manager
tells me a restraining order sets
the wrong tone, as if we were discussing
—of all things—
a story and not my life.
I am writing the poem because at first
I was turned on and I can't write
the other poem, the one about why
I am here in the first place.

Holding my father up
over the toilet
as bile thunders out of him—black, warm—
the doused ash of his body, I am writing
the poem. At the laundromat, the market,
the newsstand, I am writing the poem. When I see
the blurred photos
on the *Tribune*'s front page—
Nikki and her boyfriend—I cry
writing the poem. At the after-school
meeting, as the history teacher recounts
the gang-awareness class
he attended last Wednesday
when in fact he sat back row
in a crowd of beer-drinking men,
I am mute writing the poem. On my knees
in front of the manager, I am
writing the poem—

the last line of a villanelle—
that patterned equation of astonishing light—
night-knocking star

SPORTSMAN

That fall he taught her how to fly-
fish   said the doing of it
was like being inside
a poem   a kind of meditative grace:
he was the river
the   steelhead
the   hook.

No longer in his thrall
she knows   what it is
to be the fish
hooked out of the river
into the air
fighting   his line
and pole   gills gasping
body   bucking
on the bed
of stone
and then   the quiet
  moment   the looking
eye   to   eye
before rock
crushes bone.

TRUE GRIT

We're hurtling along the Pasadena Freeway in the diamond lane,
my brother and me, heads thrown back, laughing. Five o'clock rush hour,
windows down, ripping it. And as fast as we're going, we can still
hear the salvo of curses cast our way—

GODDAMN SHITS ASSHOLES FUCK YOU

To them we're just two reckless punks in black, speeding in a 1967 dented
Dodge ratmobile, high on angel dust, no doubt anarchists, the way we flout
the law—mosh-pit kids who can't get enough of the junk they call music
these days—the Clash, Johnny Rotten—they should all be thrown in jail.

But that's where they're wrong, it's Basie's band on the radio, and we're cranking it
full volume for our father who's in the back, comfortable now, resting on
the blue bench of Naugahyde. Of course, we're not surprised when the cop
pulls us over, informs us it's a $200 fine

for violating the three-passenger rule of the carpool lane. He scans the interior,
demands to know what's in the grocery bag, so we pull out the receipt and copper
box, open it to the twist-tied plastic baggie—five pounds fresh
from the crematorium. How can the cop argue this?

The code says nothing about bone and ash. Our father's here, goddammit,
he does exist. We've got the man in the bag, more or less.
He lets us off with a warning to heed the rules of the road, and so we drive
a polite 55 all the way home, still in the diamond lane, pissing people off.

Yet we're happy—Ellington is playing the ivories and Dad's rattling around in back, keeping time—as always—pleased to have the last laugh.

ROAD TRIP

for Maureen DeCoursey

we'd had enough of it   your dad
a sack of bones   mine a floating fine particulate
snowing on Los Angeles

wayward sisters we fled our dead & dying
left that quaking world behind   flew
up the coast in the old Dodge Dart

blue Naugahyde seats stacked with boating
gear & books   the Gipsy Kings' guitars
wailed on the radio   you rolled

a joint   we smoked it to the butt
cut our losses with each toke
lit up into late afternoon

giddy   we laughed at the great
cosmic joke   morphine drips   bedpans
spattered in bile & shit & bits

of lung   we'd seen the cells' mad savaging
our fathers come undone
anything was possible

strung out along the pavement   the wheel-flung
          roadside promenade   creatures' lives interrupted
                    in their crossing

for the next 100 miles we snapped
          photos of ourselves stopped beside the slaughter:
                    possums mice a brindled cat the flattened

stink of skunk a rat without a tail a fox
          an owl a rattlesnake a hawk   the long
                    stilled cacophony of howl & song—

what kind of daughter was I? where had I gone wrong?

the sun dropped behind the hills
          one last shot you begged   I shook my head
                    no   this was too much misery

but you insisted   swerved onto the shoulder
          & I stepped out once more   this time
                    to an oily blackened mass   impossible

to tell what it had been   yet I lay down   closed
          my eyes   let my fingers sink in   traced the blown
                    gone body   smashed bone & fur & skin

a fly's bright buzz crisscrossed my eye   padded
          the pillow of my cheek   strange tenderness
                    in the picture you took I am asleep

head tipped back to the black
dark matter   such utter
ravaged formlessness

your voice calling from far beyond
we've got to go   c'mon
& I awoke   eyes opened

to the last surrendered light   stood up   brushed
off the gravel & the grass   walked to the car
climbed in & we drove north

astonished   forsaken   windows rolled down
to the sea   FM station fading in & out
the night road's unraveling melody

MAGNITUDE 7.1

In October 1989, an earthquake registering 7.1 on the Richter scale struck the San Francisco Bay Area. It lasted 15 seconds, causing loss of life and extensive damage.

1

"Holeeeeeeee Shiiiiiit!"

'67 Dodge Dart three minutes fresh from the mechanic's

zigs—tin lunatic—into the 2

opposite lane

3

"Those assholes FUCKED my car up!"

just missing the man in the chocolate Mercedes—

4

"No insurance! I'm fucked!"—

who face pulled taut zags across the

sidewalk

5

SNAPS a fence

s t a l l s out

on a patch of green AstroTurf

"He's fucked!"

6

Slam the brakes cut the engine

run to the man

he's running toward me

7

"Son-of-a-bitch-dude's-gonna-beat-the-crap-out-of-me!"

8

(the Earth shifts her mighty hips

crosses big legs)   we both fall

hard

to the hard pavement

front teeth smash   9

"We're fucked!"

10

Look up   riddling wind blows through

the tops of elms power lines

glass chimes   11   boogie-woogie bands

of dogs bark &   H   O   W   L   cat

lightning   12

clinking rain of brick

He & I   terrified   13

hold each other

smoke ladders   to   the   b l u e   ceiling

(the Earth yawns   14

pulls her rough blanket over her

15   sleeps)

The man & I laugh   shake hands   go our separate ways

slurry of   enamel and blood—three new teeth

who cares?

"I LOVE EVERYBODY!"   new leaf

First things first: wash my mouth

NO JOKE

I try to describe my mother to my carpool partner, an ex-cop, but
I come up short. Since we're both English teachers, I rely
on allusion, our stock in trade. My mother is Medea,
Queen Gertrude, Steinbeck's Cathy burning down the house.
My carpool partner shakes her head. I try again, my own metaphors:
basket of rattlesnakes, boomslang, electric eel.
She just laughs. Clearly, she doesn't get it.

But this July day, headed east on Highway 50, it's goddamn hot,
my back wet, sticking to the seat. The windows are rolled down,
there's no relief, and I segue to my older brother's divorce—the whole sad story:
hurts, hospitals, motorcycles, madness, tracing it back to its origins,
the day of his wedding thirteen years ago, in one of those burgs
outside Los Angeles—Studio City, Glendale, Arcadia—
I'm not really sure where, but

it was late May; we'd rented a car that morning. Five of us.
My younger brother drives, my godfather in the passenger seat.
Me, my mother, and my husband in back. It's 11 o'clock.
The wedding starts at one. We're zooming on the Pasadena Freeway,
approaching the Colorado Street Bridge, when my mother launches
into a story about the overpass:

> *Built in 1919, and crossing the Arroyo Seco riverbed, it's known*
> *as the Suicide Bridge: nearly a hundred people have jumped to their deaths.*

Then she tells us another story, how one night when she was driving home

at rush hour, right near this spot, the very one we're approaching,
someone had jumped onto the freeway, traffic swerved,
as you might expect, but my mother didn't know why, after all
she hadn't seen the jumper, so she kept going, straight down
the freeway, a good 45 to 50 miles an hour in her sporty Toyota, and then
she sees him, the jumper, who is at first a body lying flat out

in the middle of her lane, but then the jumper sits up, raises his torso and head
so that he's looking directly at my mother who's driving the Toyota
45 to 50 miles an hour, but it's too late, my mother runs right over him,
the jumper, the man who is sitting up, staring into my mother's eyes,
and although she can feel the *bumpety-bump-bump* of the man's body
beneath the chassis, my mother keeps driving, not stopping, it's only
five more minutes to her house on Beech Street in South Pasadena.

At the wheel, my brother cackles. My husband and I
look to each other, astonished. I swallow and say,
"So more than likely, you killed that man." My mother snaps,
"Of course not. I never killed anyone." At that moment, my godfather,
obviously not from Los Angeles, says, "Hey, aren't we close to Dodger Stadium?"
and we move on to baseball, runs batted in, wedding gifts.

On Highway 50, to the east, thunderheads stack
fist upon fist over the Sierra.
My carpool partner nods, speechless.
Now she gets it.

INSIDE TIME PIECE WATCH & CLOCK REPAIR

A silver-haired man bends over
my mother's antique Sessions clock,
which stopped midsentence some months ago.
He speaks to the clock in dulcet tones,
turning it over, assuring my mother
that the movement can be restored.
He touches it with such tenderness
that my mother—who in the past year
has known only pain's hot forge and
brand upon her body—smiles, eyes
sparking at the possibility
that she has been given just a little
more time to set things right.

III

I praise all living, the bright and the dark.

—Thornton Wilder

KOAN

My tag. My turf. My gangland
sign. My zero. My gunfire. My empty
mind. My emperor's clothes.
My atomic wind. My blown alphabet.
My naked skin. My pawn-shop junk.
My peacock muse with his chartreuse tail.
My popinjay. My nothing pail.
My beg. My please. My dotted-line
swap with Mephistopheles.
My day-long coma. My
procrastination. My stammer.
My stutter. My inarticulation.
My absent signifier. My dead-
bird choir. My bondage.
My sin. My discipline.
My cuffs & whips. My little
apocalypse on the page.
My dugong calling. My gap-
toothed girl. My beeswaxed ears.
My oyster pearl. My gauntlet glove.
My Out-Out. My mad love-love.

GREEN ROOM, HAVASU

for V.S.

naked   we hurried upriver   before the afternoon monsoon
rolled in   leaping over rocks   loose lariats of rattlesnakes.

bold lizards—janizaries leading the way—suddenly broke
rank.   along the bank   cottonwoods and willows

gathered their green dresses up   wading to their knees.

five miles we ran   dust clouds swirled
in the air like ash.

at last we reached the falls

where thunder hollowed a deep wide pool
in the limestone travertine.

            so loud we had to shout

watch me   he yelled   *I'll guide you.*
I shivered as he dove down

swallowed in the river's booming blast.   I gulped a breath
finned behind   into a corridor emptied out of light.

blind   my heart ticked in its shell

until we bobbed into a cave   quiet   save our breathing.
unmoored   weightless asphodels   we floated.

below   the fathoms opened their turquoise doors

and like little gods we flew or fell
into the broken sky beneath the world.

GARBAGE WALK

My husband and I are wheeling out
the garbage and recycling bins
to the curbside. Stink of old flesh,
clink and rattle of tin, last week's news.
We pause to look at the moon.
Her round cheeks. A star or two
bright and glittering on the dark periphery.
We've been doing this walk together
for years. And years to come quite likely.
Then we'll stop. One before the other.
The house will pass on, fall
to its knees, or be torn down. We have
no children. Only pets, a little
graveyard of crosses. Did we ever exist?
Who can say? The moon looks on
with her kind face.

SOME DAYS

it's an hour-and-a-half commute, the highway corridor choked with car horns and exhaust, and a Dodge Ram nitwit tailgating, flashing his high beams, and I can see the man in my rear-view mirror, stabbing the air with his lit cigarette, my plain brown Toyota Corolla and its medley of bumper stickers obviously interfering with his ability to lead a life free of government, when the radio delivers nothing but bad news: extinction of the Delta smelt, home foreclosures, Santa Ana winds whipping up wildfires—some days, by the time I pull into the driveway, it's eight o'clock and dark, and all I want is to hear the pianissimo of ice clinking in a tumbler of Scotch, taste its cold burn down my throat. I turn my key in the heavy brass lock and they come running, tails straight up behind them, arching at the tip, little cataracts of purrs rumbling in their bellies, and they weave their soft bodies in and out between my legs, rubbing off the debris and dirt, singing their kind chorus of meows, burnishing me to brightness, polishing me back to the animal I am.

ODE TO AN EARTHWORM

Long pink
earth monk.
Miracle of
nonduality.
Neither he
nor she
but both.
Though
you have
no eyes,
you cry
yourself
a robe of
sticky tears.
Oyster pale,
sensitive
to light,
you work
the dark
dirt day
and night.
Five-hearted
pilgrim.
Kindred soul.
You know
the slow
world by touch

and feel—
eggshell,
coffee grounds,
apple peel—
the compost bin
your begging
bowl. Sensei.
Philosopher.
I could learn
so much
from you.
Miner of the
a priori,
nary
a thought
in your tiny
head.
You abide
in the moment's
story.
Your presence
my practice—
quickening
the dead.

PLOSIVE

This morning
after I dipped
a teabag inside my cup,
I saw the sugar
tremble in its bowl,
then quake—
up   up   up
they rose—
black swirl of ants
streaming over the rim
onto the counter,
fanning out in fury.
What giants had I waked,
how long
had they been sleeping,
I couldn't say.
I only knew
I had no time
for their little lives
and roared off
for work in the rain.
    Stalled out
on Highway 50 east,
I listen to the news
of another exploded
    bomb   strapped
to a man

in downtown traffic.
It's raining hard now,
the wipers can't keep pace.
I sip my tea and my tongue
    trips
on a tiny exoskeleton—
bitter soldier—
catches the crumb
of his dark, drowned self.
Like an undertaker
dressing the dead,
my tongue caresses
head   thorax   abdomen,
cradles him, curled
in its tip, bringing him
to the top of my mouth,
against my teeth,
as if he were an offering,
an utterance,
a word that mattered,
a multitude.

ON TEACHING

I have reached the long moment
of my life when I grieve everything.
Sorrow, my daily attendant,

dresses me in black slacks and sweater,
brushes my teeth, moves a comb
through my hair, shoves me out

the door to work where all those earnest,
expectant faces look to me
to give them something.

I don't know exactly what

I have to offer except
language—elisions and plosives swept
piecemeal and stained

off the slaughterhouse floor, transcribed
bones and sweetmeats of story I am
commissioned to place

on their tongues like the friar's tincture
and which they, in their innocence,
must swallow.

INVITATION

In deep stillness I observe my body—
its catalogue of ills—erratic heart,
crumbling bones, eyes clouded in cataracts.

Surely I was born to fall apart.

In- and exhale of breath a dance—waltz of lovers—
beautiful life, inevitable death. I am ripe
fecundity, vast portal, bright energy unleashed.

Come flies, come fishes, come beetles, come squid. Come cormorants,
herons, hawks, and shrikes. Come shrews, come moles, come mice,
come mink. Come lions, leopards, wildebeest.

Come feast! Come feast!

THUS

The whirl, the world,
the turning, the spin,
the skin I'm in, the fire,
this burning house,
the bones, the body
asunder, this boat,
the river, the rain,
the thunder, the fleeting
heart, the rhythm,
the breath, a puff
of air, a petal,
a poem, this
stepping in
to emptiness

THE KING FIRE

I tramp the dead
          dry creek bed
                    boots sinking

into ash.
          What is
                    holy here?

There are no
          visible bones—
                    I must be

breathing in their dust—
          no bodies,
                    neither squirrel scramble

nor crow caw
          or flashing white
                    rump of bounding deer.

No silver minnow
          or jumping frog.
                    No skink slipping

in underbrush. No
          bird or leafsong.
                    Only this

congregation of ghosts,
black-clacking fir
and broken

oak bowing
before a blue
unblinking eye.

MORNING BARDO

Sunday—five a.m.—the sky's dark emptiness filled
with stars. The computer humming, fat tabby purring
in my lap. I have no church to go to, no belief in God
or scripture, nothing save my body—its universe of cells
and chromosomal ladders whose rungs are snapping

and falling away even as I write. There is no ever after.

We think we know our beginnings and our endings,
our lives a story we can choose. Yet death arrives whenever,
without malice, peels back the blanket of our bodies, reveals
the burden we must carry, the one we cannot bear,
the story we are bound to lose.

WHAT AM 👁 ?

tiny
        catastrophe
                of light

briefly
        briefly
                briefly

blinking

GONEWARD

for Anne Ellen Warner (1956–2018)

This morning as the dark seeps deep into my bones
and melancholy creeps along my limbs
I ponder the daily vanishings
and the soon-to-be:

O one-horned Javan rhinoceros

I think of you who have also vanished
so suddenly—ash scattered now on the stone
of Moelwyn Mawr. How is it possible
to go on living? Can you help me

O kind-eyed Sumatran orangutan

bear the contradiction, the wedded knot
of mouse and lion,
the side-by-side
of loss and love?

O muscled mountain gorilla

Last winter you stopped by
on your way up the mountain. We stepped out
for coffee, conversation, an hour bathed
in the lumen, light, and star of you.

O scaly wondrous pangolin

We had no knowledge of melanoma already scribing
your spine and skull. When we parted, you handed me
a brown paper bag, a gift you'd picked up
on your wanderings—a jar of raw Rwandan honey.

O lovely curved vaquita

This morning I slice apples, reach into the cupboard's dark
and seek that jar, green ribbon still bowed
about its mouth. Attached, a note
in your wide, round cursive—

Life holds sweetness too.

NOVEMBER WALK

for Terry Allen

Three days before they shaved your head, wheeled you
into the operating theater,
you went walking with your oldest friends.

The cottonwood leaves were falling like gold rain.
The dogs tore ahead, tumbling
over each other, dust heaving up behind them.

You walked seven miles that morning, under the oak shadows
up and down the dun-colored hills.
You could not stop talking,

as if the tumor in your skull were a measuring cup spilling
out your life. At the river's edge
you found the snakeskin snagged

in the blackberries. Untangling it, you held the moult to the sky—
it fluttered like a translucent flag.
Carefully, you set it on the river

where it swirled in the eddy and sailed downstream over
the lip of green horizon.
Even though it was November

you shed your clothes, dove naked into the water
and disappeared
into the deep caesura.

And then the river's black door opened and you emerged
backlit by sun. You strode to shore, brown and so thin
we could count each rib.

When you shook out your hair, gold drops flew everywhere.
Each drop glistened, an upside-down world.
Somewhere, in the dead, dry grass

the snake, brown and black diamonds strewn on its back,
muscled along the earth, magnificent
in its infinite skin.

THE WHOLE TRUTH

Americans . . . need to watch what they say, watch what they do.

—Ari Fleischer, White House Press Secretary, Sept. 26, 2001

I say this: You will not corral me,
Shear my words or dock my tongue. I
Will not cut it out. My mouth is holy.
I am the human form divine. I
Promise that my broken feet
Will trample through your dreams.
I will lick your neck, your body
Politic, keep you awake. I will
Trouble your dark sleep
As you've troubled mine. I do not
Fear the wild beasts, for I am
Blessed. Black sheep, nightmare, wooly dis-
Invitation—I am the little lamb of God
Damn. God damn.

POSTMODERN

I never thought I'd live in a time like this.
Sitting at my desk to write, I can, if I like,
in just a few keystrokes, call up the grainy film
of a man's head severed by a sword. Who is this
poor man condemned to live his death, over and
over, pixelated forever on the screen? And who
are these men surrounding him, posed in black hoods,
clasping ancient weapons? Who do they think they are,
breaking and entering through the telephone wires?
They must believe I've invited them here,
into my house. And haven't I?

ŁOMAZY

I look into the picture, scrutinize the faces, the harrowed,
bent angle of the men's backs as they huddle or squat,
wait for night to fall. All of them wear newsboy caps,
wool jackets. There must be eight hundred assembled
here, on the school athletic field in the town of Łomazy.
And then there are the uniformed soldiers posted behind,
in front, and to the side—their eyes tiny black holes—
Police Battalion 101. In the back row, an officer stands
clutching a leather whip. In a short time, in the space
of a few minutes, some of the men will be marched
to the end of the town's streets, to the woods, where
they will be given shovels and spades, ordered to dig.

In the next picture, I count eleven men in a pit of their own
making. No longer wearing caps, stripped to their waists,
they throw dirt over their shoulders to the mounding piles
surrounding them. They are sweating in the midday sun.
They are probably not aware that Lieutenant Gnade is taking
this photograph. But the men understand that soon enough
they will be dead, everyone shot in the back of the head
by the drunk-on-vodka Trawnikis, who've been trucked in
from the Ukraine to spare the German soldiers nightmares.

I focus on one man whose trousers sag off his body. I can see
the white, narrow band of his underwear. He cannot know
that a woman is watching him sixty years in the future
from the safety of her bed. This man has no idea that his singular

figure will always be stooping, bending to the earth as if he were about to fall to his knees in prayer, and I am joining him there.

EROSION

for the missing women of Ciudad Juárez

We are the lost and grieved.
Now the earth our mother.
The wind and rain our sisters.
The waltzing mouse, fire ant, mole,
the horned toad, spider
    all sisters.

Each day we are undressed
and blessed to our bones.
Bit by bit. We articulate
from the dust. Ribs, tibias,
femurs rise to stand. Refuse
    your idea of us.

Ulnas, metacarpals
extend across years,
across desert, the city,
las maquiladoras,
the courtroom—point to you.
    Acusamos.

RSVP

for the lost and displaced of Marwahin, Lebanon, July 2006

Forgive me for not responding until now,
but I would like to pause for a moment to acknowledge
your act of kindness: your aerial distribution of leaflets
warning the villagers to flee—the elders so deft with their canes,
the wounded in their swift wheelchairs, and the families
with little children and pets—who knows what they're up to—
their belongings crushed into suitcases and wagons.
It's so good of you to consider them before you drop the bombs.
I'm sure they're grateful as they exodus en masse
along the rubbled highways. And thankful too
for the border closures on all sides so they can be rounded up,
herded to exactly where you want them. After all,
this is their lament, centuries old—this is their home,
and home, as you know so well, is where the heart is.
So forgive me for not responding sooner, but given
these circumstances, I am speechless.

POLYPHEMUS

Antheraea polyphemus

This July night I answer an insistent knocking at my door.
I find her felled and wheeling on the burlap mat,
heaving in fits and starts, ragged wings thrumming.

Kneeling, I cup her in my hands, feel the silk fur
of antennae, soft whir of torn beauty. Has she
mated? How much of life is left?

I sense she is summoning up her force, what Schopenhauer calls
the will. Delicate creature, only a gram in my palm, a mote,
even she is compelled to right the world,

to move with or against the light. What am I

to her or she to me? Seraphim? Ephemerata? What form
does she embody? Could she be my long dead father?
For I have seen him like this late at night

collapsed on the bathroom mat, heaving, then utterly spent. Still,
each morning he willed himself up to coffee, cigarettes, walked
whistling to the bus stop, and on to work and his short life.

Is it the will, then, that steers me down the driveway this moonless night
to the road where I unfold my hands, lift her to the stars?
Fly, I command, god that I am, savior to something.

AUTUMN

The satyr is here again. Invisible,
he skips through the backyard orchard
shaking apples from the tree, undressing
figs. The pistachios offer themselves,
crack open their shells. Everywhere now,
all at once, he delights in thinning down
the world with his want. He dances
up the hill until he arrives at my side,
breath on my neck. Hair whirling
about my head, heart galloping
in its cage. Twilight. Winter's ache
in my bones and snow is coming. I am
ready for flight. Blow, wind, blow.

BASHO THE SKUNK

All winter he's journeyed, wandering roads,
burrowing under fences and spaces
in between. His nose an alms bowl—
snuffling out compost, trash cans, traces
of accidental kindness. And here he is now,
poised on my back stair, stamping his feet,
thick-plumed tail arching, cowling
his dark eyes. It is his nature to greet
me thus—his form not separate
from his given self. Mind and body
unified, he does not question the state
of his existence. The world is purely
pungent scent, this naked moment
of clarity—flowering, impermanent.

PRAISE

In the eye of the elephant, in the eye of the mouse, in the dark and the bright,
in the moon and sun, in the neutrino's flight, in the electron's spin,
in the universe expanding out or folding in, in yang and yin, in miniature,
in magnitude, in melancholy, in gratitude, in silence and in bliss,
in the Golden Mean of the nautilus, in the Boolean laptop, in tongues untied
in the barbaric yawp—love abides. In summer heat and winter hail,
in the amoeba, in the great blue whale, on the mountain crest, in the valley
swale, in taut muscle, in crumbling bone, in thunderheads, in river stone—
love abides. In Galileo and Gogol, in St. Augustine and Sartre,
in the magical mind, in the miracle heart, halfway through morning,
in midafternoon, in the quark, in the quasar, in the rush, in the swoon,
in the spark—love abides. In the spiraling arms of the Milky Way,
in Andromeda, in night and day, in the owl and the bear, in fur and feather,
in prayer—love abides. In the dance, love abides. In the dance, in the dance,
in the coming and going, in the blue shift and red, in light and gravity,
in the living and the dead, in the madeleine of memory, in the house of pain,
in joy, in suffering—love abides. On the sloop in the sound, on the raft
on the river, in the dance, in headwinds, in yaw, in the following sea, in brio
and humility, in surrendering. In the carmine evening, in the chartreuse
dawn, in the desert, in the dingle, in the robin's song, in the humid streets
of Brooklyn, on bicycles, in bare feet, on BlackBerrys, in taxis, in the bitter-
sweet—love abides. In Limerick and Lotus, in Sally's soothsaying dream,
in turquoise heels, on the walk on the trail, in the wedding dress, in the dry
castanets of the rattlesnake's tail, in thistle and vetch—love abides.
In the breath of the earth, in the wind, in the rising and falling and rising
again, in the gathering, in family and friends, in the wild tribe whooping
beneath the wild tree—love abides. In the earth's dervish around the sun,

where you are now in time undone, in the golden string, in the coming
and going of everything, in the oak's craggy limbs, in the blue bowl
of sky, in the boundless river, in your luminous eyes, in your being,
in the dance, in your kiss—love abides.

NOTES

Walt Whitman epigraph: "I stand and look at them long and long" is a line from Whitman's poem "Song of Myself, 32."

In "Eye and the Elephant," "*Hatti Hatti mero saathi*" is a Nepali expression meaning "Elephant Elephant my friend."

"Hippopotamus: An Inserted Proposition": The epigraph is taken from an article that first appeared in *The Southern Journal of Philosophy* in 1993.

The pika that figures in "The Vanishing" is the American pika that has disappeared from a 64-square-mile span of habitat in Northern California's Sierra Nevada. This local extinction is a result of climate change.

Billie Holiday epigraph: "Good morning heartache, sit down" is the final line from Billie Holiday's signature song "Good Morning Heartache." Irene Higginbotham, Ervin Drake, and Dan Fisher wrote the lyrics.

"He Drank Because": Jerry & Johnny's is the name of a San Francisco newspaper bar on Third Street where *San Francisco Examiner* news reporters hung out in the '50s and '60s.

"Losing It" borrows lyrics from the Ohio Players' song "Skin Tight."

Thornton Wilder epigraph: "I praise all living, the bright and the dark" is a line spoken by Pamphilus, a main character in Wilder's novel *The Woman of Andros*.

"Green Room, Havasu" is inspired by a long-ago hike up Havasu Creek, a body of water sacred to the Havasupai people and a tributary of the Colorado River.

"Plosive" speaks to the January 29, 2004, Gaza Street bus bombing in Rehavia, Jerusalem.

"The King Fire" refers to the 2014 wildfire that burned over 97,000 acres in El Dorado County, California.

"Goneward" is for zoologist Anne Warner and the vanishing animal species she worked to save.

"The Whole Truth" is after William Blake.

The scene described in "Łomazy" is drawn from Daniel Jonah Goldhagen's book *Hitler's Willing Executioners*.

"Praise" is an epithalamium written to commemorate Doug and Rebecca Foster on their wedding day.

ACKNOWLEDGMENTS

Grateful acknowledgment is made to the following publications in which many of these poems, some in slightly different forms, previously appeared:

Alehouse: "On Teaching"; *The Bark*: "This Hound"; *Bindweed*: "At Martin Angel's"; *Boatman's Quarterly*: "Green Room, Havasu"; *California Fire & Water* (Story Street Press, 2020): "The Vanishing"; *Canary*: "The King Fire," "Owling," "Road Trip"; *The Ear*: "Erosion"; *Fine Madness*: "How I Grew Up"; *Flint Hills Review*: "Postmodern"; *Gathering Rounds, Volume 2* (Sirensong Publishing, 2022): "What Am 👁 ?"; *Hanging Loose*: "Death Deluxe," "Magnitude 7.1," "Mom Drives Fast," "True Grit"; *Horned Things*: "Herself"; *In Posse Review*: "Koan"; *Insight Journal*: "Basho the Skunk," "Invitation"; *Manzanita*: "Autumn," "Thanksgiving"; *Margie*: "RSVP"; *O Magazine*: "Bodhisattva"; *The Pedestal*: "Praise"; *Poetry Now*: "Sportsman"; *Red Wheelbarrow*: "Eye and the Elephant"; *Rhino*: "After the Election"; *Runes*: "Garbage Walk," "Plosive"; *Sacramento News & Review*: "The Whole Truth"; *The San Francisco Bay Guardian*: "Cockeyed," under the title "Kansas 1960"; *Scapegoat Review*: "Łomazy"; *South Dakota Review*: "Requiem"; *Southern California Review*: "Sunday"; *Spillway*: "Hippopotamus: An Inserted Proposition," "Inside Time Piece Watch & Clock Repair," "Polyphemus"; *The Spoon River Poetry Review*: "Confession"; *Suisun Valley Review*: "Morning Bardo," "No Joke"; *Susurrus*: "He Drank Because"; *Talking River Review*: "Work"; *Tor House Newsletter*: "November Walk"; *Tule Review*: "Ode to an Earthworm"; *West Trestle Review*: "Some Days"; *What's Nature Got to Do with Me?* (Native West Press, 2011): "Apparition"

A number of poems in this book appeared in the chapbook *He Drank Because* (Rattlesnake Press, 2008).

"Łomazy" received a National Honorable Mention in the 2021 Joe Gouveia Outermost Poetry Contest sponsored by WOMR: Outermost Community Radio.

"November Walk" received an Honorable Mention in the 2011 Robinson Jeffers Tor House Poetry Prize contest.

"On Teaching" received *Alehouse's* Grand Prize 2010 Happy Hour Poetry Award.

"After the Election" received a second-place Editors' Prize in *Rhino* 2008 and third place in Sacramento's 2005 Focus on Writers contest.

"Confession" was selected as one of two runner-ups in the 2003 *Spoon River Poetry Review* Editors' Prize Contest.

"Cockeyed," under the title "Kansas 1960," was awarded first place in the 1995 *San Francisco Bay Guardian* Poetry Contest.

"Apparition" was reprinted in *Deep Wild* and *Halfway to Halfway and Back: More River Stories* (Halfway Publishing, 2019).

"Bodhisattva" and a five-line passage from "Autumn" were set to chorale music by composer Stacey Philipps in *Gathering Rounds, Volume 2* (Sirensong Publishing, 2024).

"Confession" was reprinted in the *Cloud View Poets Anthology* (Arctos Press, 2005).

"Death Deluxe" and "Mom Drives Fast" were reprinted in *Slipstream.*

"Garbage Walk" was reprinted in *Verse Daily*.

"Green Room, Havasu" was reprinted in *Halfway to Halfway and Back: More River Stories*.

Big thanks to Brett Hall Jones and the Community of Writers for the mountain air and scholarship assistance that gave rise to many of these poems, and to the folks at Sixteen Rivers Press for guidance, community, and wisdom. I am also grateful to the many souls who brought this book into being: Dr. Marian Birch, for her years of wise, calm counsel; the Cloud View poets, who for years gathered in the name of beauty and fire—especially Susan Terris, for her boundless support; 'Lyn Follett, who opened her heart and home to me and so many other poets; and mentor David St. John, whose critiques and encouragement made me think I wasn't a straight-up fool for writing poetry.

A shout-out, too, to the following teachers and friends who were instrumental in the crafting of these poems and this book: English teacher Dennis Mele (I never forgot you!); the late Stanley Plumly, for taking me under his wing, shaking me out of my shyness, and introducing me to the work of Sharon Olds; Molly Fisk, who helped me find my way back to poetry; Rose Black, for her brilliance; Connie Corzilius Spasser, whose grit and talent have been a necessary spark; Shawn Pittard, for twenty-plus years of poeming and conversation; bad girls Francesca Bell and Christina Hutchins, for their bone-rattling good poems; April Ossmann, for her insights; poetry maven Kathy Kieth, for Rattlesnake Press; the Sacramento Friday Night Writers—Brad Buchanan, Frank Graham, Tim Kahl, Penny Kline, and Richard Lopez—for our raucous monthly rendezvous; my students at Sacramento City College, whose stories, boldness, and honesty moved me every day; my Sacramento City College colleagues Albert Garcia, Jeff Knorr, Ginny McReynolds, and Danny Romero, for their esprit de corps; the poets of Red Fox Underground—Patricia Caspers, Taylor Graham, Carol Lynn Stevenson Grellas, Lara Gularte, Irene Lipshin, Carol Louise Moon, Brigit Truex, Jen Vernon, Kate Wells, and Wendy Patrice Williams—for our Sunday-morning poetry jams; Robin Center, Rebecca Lawton, Katie Rutherford, Mark Shaw, Dan Silverberg, and Andie Thrams, for having my back; my Oakland goils Janan Apaydin, Diane Remoundakis, Jennifer Williams Taylor, and the late Anne Warner for being in my corner since fourth grade; the Sierra Insight and South Fork sanghas, for keeping me on the middle path; and the late Leigh Fortson—soul sister and wild seed—for her love and joie de vivre.

As well, gratitude goes out to all the rivers I've known and guides I've boated with, foremost among them Dick Linford and Joe Daly, who as owners of Echo River Trips made my life on rivers possible. Without their patience and the big-hearted river community they raised up, there would be no poems. Period.

Lastly, I am indebted to my families—my family of origin: my brothers Jed and Sean Belcher, who've lived inside many of these poems as much as I have, and my father and mother, Jerry and Nancy Belcher, both writers, long gone, who would have been perturbed but proud to see this collection published—and the Magneson murmuration, who welcomed me into their enormous, ever-expanding family of artists, writers, river guides, educators, and dairy farmers; and most of all to my husband, Eric, my first and best reader and keeper of my heart.

ABOUT THE AUTHOR

Over the years, Moira Magneson has worked as a river guide, artist's model, truck driver, television writer, editor, and community college writing instructor. A Northern California native, she lives in the Sierra foothills where she has spearheaded many art actions and initiatives, including El Dorado County's Poetry Out Loud Competition, Veterans' Voices, Barbaric Yawp, and Black Lives: An American Overture. In 2024, she was the poet in residence for ForestSong, a community arts project exploring solastalgia, biophilia, and resilience in the face of wildfire devastation. Magneson is the author of *A River Called Home: A River Fable*, an illustrated novella (Toad Road Press, 2024). *In the Eye of the Elephant* is her first full-length collection of poems.

Sixteen Rivers Press is a shared-work, nonprofit poetry collective dedicated to providing an alternative publishing avenue for Northern California poets. Founded in 1999 by seven writers, the press is named for the sixteen rivers that flow into San Francisco Bay.

SAN JOAQUIN • FRESNO • CHOWCHILLA • MERCED • TUOLUMNE
STANISLAUS • CALAVERAS • BEAR • MOKELUMNE • COSUMNES
AMERICAN • YUBA • FEATHER • SACRAMENTO • NAPA • PETALUMA